To

Jasper Andrew

on the occasion of his

Baptism

on

3rd August 2013

with love

Philip + Wendy

x

My Little Bible

Drawn and retold
by George & Angie Allen

kevin
mayhew

First published in 2006
This edition published in 2007 by

KEVIN MAYHEW LTD
Buxhall, Stowmarket, Suffolk, IP14 3BW
E-mail: info@kevinmayhewltd.com
Website: www.kevinmayhew.com

© 2006 George & Angie Allen

The right of George & Angie Allen to be identified as the authors
of this work has been asserted by them in accordance with the Copyright,
Designs and Patents Act, 1988.

No part of this publication may be reproduced, stored in a retrieval system,
or transmitted, in any form or by any means, electronic, mechanical, photocopying,
recording or otherwise, without the prior written permission of the publisher.

All rights reserved.

9 8 7 6 5 4 3 2 1 0

Hardback: ISBN 978 184417 728 8
Catalogue No. 1500972

Paperback: ISBN 978 184417 727 1
Catalogue No. 1500973

Artwork by George & Angie Allen
Design by Chris Coe

Printed and bound in India

Contents ... the Old Testament

Contents ... the New Testament

Introduction

We hope you enjoy
these Bible stories.
They are from
our favourite book.
We love them
and hope you do too.

For
Nadia, Cherine and Jodie,
our inspiration

Genesis	Ecclesiastes
Exodus	Song of Songs
Leviticus	Isaiah
Numbers	Jeremiah
Deuteronomy	Lamentations
Joshua	Ezekiel
Ruth	Daniel
Judges	Hosea
1 Samuel	Joel
2 Samuel	Amos
1 Kings	Obadiah
2 Kings	Jonah
1 Chronicles	Micah
Ezra	Nahum
Nehemiah	Habakkuk
Esther	Zephaniah
Job	Haggai
Psalms	Zechariah
Proverbs	Malachi

The Creation

In the beginning, everything was dark.

God said, 'Let there be light.'
God made the sun for the day,
and the gentler moon for the night.

Then God separated out
land, sea and sky,
and filled them with animals,
fish and birds.

God made the first man and woman
and every plant and tree and
was pleased with what he had done.

Then he rested on the seventh day.

Genesis 1–2:3

9

Adam and Eve

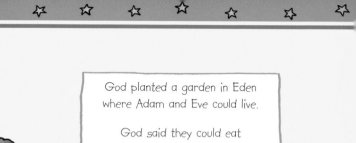

God planted a garden in Eden
where Adam and Eve could live.

God said they could eat
from any tree except one.

So the crafty snake tricked them
into eating from it;
he told Eve that the fruit
would give them power like God's.

Adam and Eve both ate the fruit.
So God sent them out
of the garden for ever.

Genesis 2:8–3:24

Noah's Ark

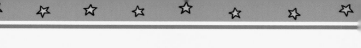

God told Noah to build an ark,
because there was going to be a flood.

Noah loaded it with two
of all living creatures.

It rained for forty days and nights,
flooding the earth.

After the flood had dried out,
Noah left the ark.

God put a rainbow in the sky
to show his promise never to destroy
the world with water again.

Genesis 6:11–9:17

The tower of Babel

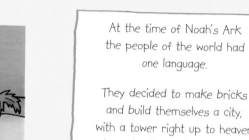

At the time of Noah's Ark
the people of the world had
one language.

They decided to make bricks
and build themselves a city,
with a tower right up to heaven
to make themselves famous.

God wanted them to spread
throughout the world
so he gave them many languages.

Genesis 11:1-9

15

Abraham and Sarah

Abraham and Sarah
had lots of sheep, but no children.

God promised Abraham
that his family would be as many
as the stars in the sky, but Abraham
didn't even have one child!

But he kept believing what God had
promised and when Sarah was old,
she had a baby son, Isaac.

Genesis 21:1-7

Abraham and Isaac

God gave Abraham one son, Isaac.

To test Abraham's faith
God asked Abraham
to sacrifice Isaac.

Abraham built an altar
on which to kill Isaac.

But then God said to him,
'Do not harm Isaac,
I know you love me.'

So instead Abraham killed a ram
that was caught in a nearby bush.

Genesis 22:1-13

19

Rebekah

Abraham wanted his son,
Isaac, to have a wife,
so he sent his servant back
to their own country to find one.

Beside a well,
the servant asked a local woman,
Rebekah, for a drink.

The woman pulled up water for him,
and some more for his ten camels.

The servant knew that she was the
wife God had chosen for Isaac.

Genesis 24:1-67

Jacob and Esau

Isaac and Rebekah had twin sons,
Jacob and Esau.

Although they were twins,
they did not look alike and their
interests and skills were different.

Jacob was his mother's favourite
and loved to do things at home.

Esau was his father's favourite
and loved to be out hunting in the wild.

Genesis 25:19-28

Jacob's dream

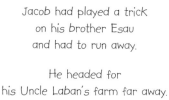

Jacob had played a trick
on his brother Esau
and had to run away.

He headed for
his Uncle Laban's farm far away.

On the way, he slept
and dreamed of a ladder
set up from earth to heaven.

Angels were going up and down it.

Then God said to him,
'I will always be with you
and give you a home of your own.'

Genesis 28:10-15

25

Joseph's angry brothers

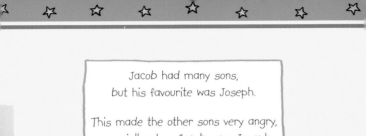

Jacob had many sons,
but his favourite was Joseph.

This made the other sons very angry,
especially when Jacob gave Joseph
a beautiful coat with long sleeves.

Joseph had a dream
that one day all his brothers
would bow down to him.

That made his brothers hate him
all the more, and try to harm him.

But they just helped
the dream come true!

Genesis 37:1-11

27

Baby Moses

The cruel King of Egypt wanted to kill
all the Israelite boy babies.

So Moses' mother hid him
in the bulrushes, and his big sister,
Miriam, kept watch.

The King's daughter found Moses and
took him to the palace to care for him.

Miriam thought quickly, and offered
to find an Israelite woman
to be the baby's nurse.

So Moses' mother was able
to look after him at the palace!

Exodus 2:1-10

Moses and the plagues

Moses grew up caring about
the Israelite people who were
treated horribly in Egypt.

God appeared to him in a fire
that lit up a bush but,
miraculously, didn't burn it.

God said, 'Go and tell the wicked King
to let my people go,
or I'll give him real trouble –
I'll turn the water into blood and send
plagues of horrible insects and frogs,
and it will be dreadful.'

The King still refused
to let the people go.

Exodus 3:1–8:30

31

The Red Sea

When God's people left Eygpt,
Pharoah the King
sent an army to stop them.

When they arrived at the Red Sea
they had nowhere to go
to escape the army.

God told Moses to hold up
his special staff over the sea.
The sea parted so that they could
pass through on dry land.

The Egyptian army followed them
but the sea came back
and drowned them all.

Exodus 14:5–28

33

Moses strikes the rock

When God freed the slaves,
Moses led them across the desert
toward the promised land.

Soon, they started to complain
because they had no water to drink.

God had promised
to give them all they needed.

He told Moses
to hit a rock with his stick,
and out came water
for them to drink.

Exodus 17:1-7

God makes the rules

God called Moses
up the high mountain.

The mountain was covered
with thunderclouds.

There, God gave him two stone slabs
with some rules written on them,
to help the people live more happily.

Moses took them down
for the people to read,
and they became known as
the Ten Commandments.

Exodus 19:1-25; 31:18

37

Joshua and Caleb went as spies
to check out the land
God had promised to Moses.

They brought back giant grapes
to show how wonderful the land was.

'Let's go and live in the land now,'
they said. Some of
the other spies disagreed –
they were scared and didn't fully
believe God's promise.

Numbers 13:16–14:10

Jericho's walls come down

The Israelite people had to get into Jericho – but the city had high walls and locked gates.

God told Joshua and the people of Israel to march round the walls once a day, for six days.

On the seventh day they marched round the city seven times. The seventh time the religious leaders blew their trumpets the people shouted out.

Then the walls came tumbling down.

Joshua 6:1-27

Ruth and Boaz

When her husband died
Ruth stayed with her mother-in-law
instead of returning to her own family.

She didn't know anyone
in the field where she worked. She
was new in town and would have felt
a little afraid.

Even so she worked very hard,
and picked enough grain to feed
herself and her mother-in-law Naomi.

The owner of the field
also saw how hard she worked.

His name was Boaz,
and Ruth later became his wife.

Ruth 2:1-23

Samson and Delilah

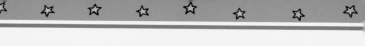

God gave Samson the gift
of great strength.

His wife Delilah – who was
secretly plotting with his enemies –
discovered that the secret of
Samson's strength lay in his long hair.

She cut it off to make Samson weak,
and handed him over to his enemies.

But as his hair began to grow again,
Samson's strength returned
and he was able to pull down
their temple with his bare hands.

Judges 16:1-31

Samuel's calling

When Samuel was a boy
he lived in the temple.

He even slept inside the temple.

One night God called out to him.

Samuel thought that
it was Eli the priest calling him.

But after the third time
Eli the priest told him it must be God!

Samuel waited for God
to call him again and
this time he listened carefully
to what God had to say.

1 Samuel 3:1-10

Tall Saul

The Israelites didn't have a king –
the prophet Samuel told them
what God wanted to happen.

But the people weren't satisfied
with this and wanted a king.

God was sad about it,
and advised against it,
but when they kept on asking
he showed Samuel who to choose –
a tall handsome king: Saul.

1 Samuel 8:1–9:2

49

David and Goliath

Young David was minding the sheep
when his father told him
to take some food to his brothers;
they were soldiers about to go
into battle against the Philistines.

The Philistines had a giant called
Goliath fighting for them,
and the Israelites were frightened.

David had a slingshot for scaring off
wild animals that came after the sheep.

He used that to defeat Goliath
and win the battle.

1 Samuel 17:1-50

51

David and Saul

King Saul chased David.

He wanted to kill him
out of jealousy and anger.

David was hiding from Saul in a
very large cave when Saul came in.

David did not take the opportunity
to kill Saul and only cut off
the corner of his cloak.

David showed respect for the king.

1 Samuel 24:1-12

King Ahab

King Ahab was a very bad man.

He didn't trust God for all he needed.

Instead he bowed down to a man
carved on a stone and asked for rain
to make the plants grow.

How silly,
of course no rain came.

(Elijah prayed to God and the rain fell.)

1 Kings 16:29-33

55

Elijah's fire

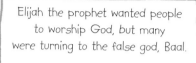

Elijah the prophet wanted people
to worship God, but many
were turning to the false god, Baal.

One day, Baal's prophets
were trying to burn some meat
as a sacrifice to Baal.

They prayed for hours that Baal
would send fire to their altar,
but nothing happened.

Then Elijah set up his sacrifice and
prayed a short, simple prayer to God
who sent fire and burned it up –
even though water
had been poured on it.

1 Kings 18:22-39

David and the temple

King David wanted very much
to build a temple for God.

But God told David:
'No! It will be your son Solomon
who will build the temple.'

Then David had a great idea.

He could prepare the things
needed to build it.

He selected the finest wood and
provided gold, bronze and silver.

He also chose priests
to look after the temple.

1 Chronicles 22:2-19

59

Esther

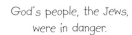

God's people, the Jews,
were in danger.

Haman, a nobleman in the King's court,
had tricked him into passing a law
which was going to kill them all!

Esther was the King's wife, the queen.

She was very beautiful and brave and
she told the King about Haman's plot.

She made sure God's people
were saved and that
God's enemies died.

Esther 1-10

The furnace

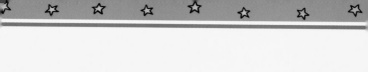

The King was very angry
with Daniel's three friends Shadrach,
Meshach and Abednego.

They wouldn't bow and worship
the statue that he had made!

So the King threw them
into a very hot furnace.

But instead of being burnt up,
God rescued them!

The King was amazed and praised God.

Daniel 3:13-30

Daniel and the lions

Daniel always worshipped God
and not the King's idols.

This was against the law.

So the King threw Daniel
into a cage filled with hungry lions.

Because God was with Daniel,
the lions did not eat him up.

When the King saw this
he began to worship God as well.

Daniel 6:13-26

Jonah and the giant fis

God told Jonah to go to Nineveh and tell the people to stop doing wrong.

Jonah didn't want to do that, so he got on a ship going the other way.

A terrifying storm almost sank the ship, and Jonah realised he couldn't hide from God.

'Throw me overboard,' he said, 'and the storm will stop.'

God sent a giant fish to swallow Jonah and carry him to dry land.

So Jonah went to Nineveh after all!

Jonah 1:1-17

Matthew	1 Timothy
Mark	2 Timothy
Luke	Titus
John	Philemon
The Acts	Hebrews
Romans	James
1 Corinthians	1 Peter
2 Corinthians	2 Peter
Galatians	1 John
Ephesians	2 John
Philippians	3 John
Colossians	Jude
1 Thessalonians	Revelation
2 Thessalonians	

The
New Testament

Mary and the angel

Mary was startled
when an angel came to her home.

'Don't be afraid,' said the
angel Gabriel, 'I have good news.
You are going to have a very special
baby and you will call him Jesus.'

Mary was surprised.

The angel went on: 'Your cousin
Elizabeth will soon have a baby too.
These things are all part
of God's plan.'

Then the angel was gone.

Luke 1:26-33

Jesus is born

Joseph and Mary were visitors
in Bethlehem, just at the time
Jesus was to be born, and they
couldn't find anywhere to stay.

The only shelter
they could find was a stable.

When the baby Jesus was born,
Mary used the manger that the
animals ate from as a cradle.

Luke 2:4-7

73

John the Baptiser

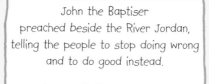

John the Baptiser
preached beside the River Jordan,
telling the people to stop doing wrong
and to do good instead.

The people listened to him,
and he baptised them –
a kind of washing, to show that
they were making a new,
clean start in life.

He told the people to expect
a greater person than him – Jesus.

Jesus came to the Jordan
to be baptised by John.

Matthew 3:1-15

Water into wine

Jesus and his disciples
went to a wedding with his mother.

The people hosting the wedding
ran out of wine and so Jesus' mother
asked him to help.

He told the servants
to fill up six water jars with water
and then offer some
to the master of the banquet.

When he tasted the water,
it had turned into the best wine.

Jesus had turned the water into wine.

John 2:1-11

77

The catch of fish

Peter and John had been fishing
all night long with their friends.

They had caught nothing.
Jesus told them to put
into deep water and try again.

When they did,
they caught lots of big fish.

They were astonished.

Jesus told them,
'From now on you will catch men.'

So they left everything
and followed him.

Luke 5:4-11

The twelve special friends

Jesus used a lot of friends
to help him spread the good news.

From those, he chose twelve
to be *especially* close to him
and prepare to carry on his work.

They became known as 'the Twelve',
and later were called 'Apostles'.

The Twelve left what they were doing
and gave their lives to following
and learning from Jesus.

Mark 3:13-19

The sick man healed

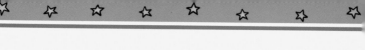

Jesus was healing many sick people.

Some men brought
their friend for healing.

The man was so sick
he was still on his bed.

They couldn't get into the house
where Jesus was as there were
too many people.

So they lowered him down
through the roof of the house,
and Jesus healed him.

Luke 5:18-26

The sower

Jesus told a story about a farmer
who sowed seed in his field.

Some of the seed couldn't grow
because it landed on stones,
or was eaten by hungry birds,
or choked by weeds,
but the rest grew into a huge harvest.

Jesus said that teaching people about
God is like sowing seeds in their minds.

Sometimes nothing comes of it,
but at other times
it grows into wonderful faith.

Mark 4:3-8

The storm

Jesus and his friends
were crossing the lake in a boat.

Jesus was fast asleep.

Suddenly there were very big waves.

The friends were very frightened,
but Jesus stayed asleep.

In the end they woke Jesus
and he stopped the storm.

Jesus said that they should trust
in God and not be afraid.

Mark 4:35-41

Houses built on rock and san

Jesus often taught using stories
that were easy to understand.

For example, he told about two men,
both building houses.

One built his house on rock,
but the other chose sand because
it was easier to dig the foundations.

After a big storm, only the house
on the rock was still standing.

Jesus told the people that
following his teachings is like building
our lives on solid rock foundations.

Matthew 7:24-27

89

The sick girl healed

The rich man's daughter was very sick.

Even with all his money,
he couldn't find a doctor to heal her.

'I know,' he thought,
'I'll ask Jesus to heal her.'

Before Jesus got there
she had died,
but Jesus told her to wake up –
and to everyone's amazement
she did!

Matthew 9:18-26

Feeding the 5000

Many, many people had come
to listen to Jesus.

They sat for hours listening to him,
and now they were hungry.

There was nothing to eat except
a boy's lunch of some fish and bread.

Jesus blessed the food and
shared it amongst the people.

Everyone had their fill
and they even had a lot left over.

John 6:5-13

93

Walking on water

Jesus sent his disciples
to a town across the lake.
He went away somewhere
to be quiet and to pray.

The disciples were on the lake
in the middle of the night
when Jesus caught up with them.

He had walked across the lake
to be where they were.

The disciples were amazed.
Jesus was walking on water!

Matthew 14:22-27

95

The lost sheep

Jesus told the story
about a shepherd who had
one hundred sheep to look after.

It so happened that one sheep got lost
and was far away from all the others.

The shepherd left the ninety-nine sheep
and went and found the lost one.

God loves and cares for us
just as this shepherd
loved and cared for that sheep.

Matthew 18:12-14

97

The surprising Samaritan

A wounded man
lay by the side of the road.
He had been beaten and robbed
by some bad men.

First a priest went past,
and then a Levite who he thought
might have helped him;
both saw him but hurried away.

Then a traveller stopped
and took care of him.

What surprised the man was that
the traveller who helped him was a
Samaritan – and he'd always thought
they were bad people!

Luke 10:30-35

Mary and Martha

Mary and Martha were sisters
who welcomed Jesus to their home.

A meal had to be prepared
and the house tidied.

Martha was very angry
because Mary sat listening to Jesus
while Martha was working hard
preparing the dinner.

But Mary knew that it was better
to listen and learn first
while Jesus was teaching.

Luke 10:38-42

The lost son

Jesus told the story of a young man
who asked his dad for lots of money,
and then went to a faraway land
and wasted it all.

Now he was very poor and lonely,
and decided to go back home.

He thought his dad
would be terribly cross
but his dad was so happy to see him
that he threw a party!

Luke 15:11-32

Jesus comes to dinner

Zacchaeus collected taxes for the Romans who had taken over the land.

The local people hated the Romans, and everyone who worked for them.

Zacchaeus wanted to see Jesus, but was too short to see over the crowd that had gathered – so he climbed a tree.

Jesus called out to him: 'Today, I'm coming to your house for dinner.'

Zacchaeus was excited; most people wouldn't even speak to him, but Jesus was coming to dinner!

Luke 19:1-6

Let the children come

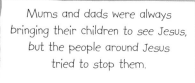

Mums and dads were always
bringing their children to see Jesus,
but the people around Jesus
tried to stop them.

They said:
'Jesus is too busy for children!'

But Jesus told them:
'Don't stop them,
let the children come
because they're really important.'

Mark 10:13-16

A blind man healed

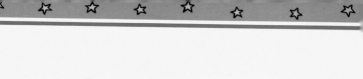

Bartimaeus couldn't see at all.

He was blind
and sat begging for money.

When he heard Jesus coming his way
he was very excited.

He called out as loudly as he could.

He knew Jesus could make him see.

When Jesus heard him calling,
he came and healed him straightaway.

Mark 10:46-52

The **money changers**

Jesus went into the temple
to pray and worship God.

In the temple courts
he found men selling things
and changing money
on tables as if at a market.

'The temple is for prayer,'
he said, 'not to shop.'

So Jesus overturned their tables
and drove them out.

John 2:13-16

Lazarus

Jesus' friend Lazarus was sick.

His friends called for Jesus to come
but when he arrived Lazarus
had been dead for three days.

The friends were very sad,
and said, 'If you had been here
he would have lived.'

Jesus went to the cave
where his body lay
and made him alive again.

John 11:1–12:19

Palm Sunday

Jesus asked his friends
to bring him a donkey,
one that had never been ridden.

He was going to ride into Jerusalem.

Many people waving palm branches
had come to welcome
Jesus along the road.

They shouted out that Jesus
was a great King who
had come to save them.

Mark 11:1-11

115

The Last Supper

Jesus met with his friends just before
he was to die on the cross.

He had a simple meal with them
in which they shared
some bread and wine.

Jesus said:
Please think of me when I'm gone,
and repeat this simple meal:

Just a small piece of bread
and a sip of wine,
until I come back.

Luke 22:14-22; 1 Corinthians 11:23-26

Jesus on the cross

Jesus' enemies had made up stories
about him to get him put to death,
and he was nailed to a cross
along with other prisoners.

Most of his friends ran away
but his mother and his
closest friends stayed with him.

Even in his terrible pain, Jesus forgave
the people who were hurting him.

When he died,
they thought it was all over,
but an amazing thing
was going to happen.

John 19:16-27

Easter Day

Very early on Easter Sunday
some women went to the tomb
where Jesus' body had been laid.

They wanted to look after the body,
but the tomb was empty.

They were amazed
because Jesus had gone and instead
they found an angel who said:
'Jesus isn't here.
He has risen!'

Matthew 28:1-6

Ascension

When Jesus had finished everything
on earth that his Father
had told him to do,
he went back to heaven.

Jesus went up into the sky
and was hidden by the clouds.

His disciples looked up
into the sky and was amazed!

Two angels came and said:
'Why are you looking into the sky?
Jesus will return one day in just
the same way as you saw him go!'

Acts 1:9-11

Pentecost

The followers of Jesus
kept meeting together
after Jesus went back into heaven.

He had told them
that soon the Holy Spirit
would come upon them.

One day a powerful wind
shook their meeting place and fire
seemed to rest on each person.

All of them praised God
and they began
to speak different languages;
the Holy Spirit had come upon them!

Acts 2:1-4

Paul and Silas

Paul and Silas were arrested
for telling everyone about Jesus.

Soldiers put them in chains
deep inside a prison.

Paul kept singing and praying
to God late into the night.

And so at midnight
an earthquake set them free!

The jailer was very amazed
and he became a Christian.

Acts 16:16-33